RICCO FRANCIS

FROM PAIN TO LOVE

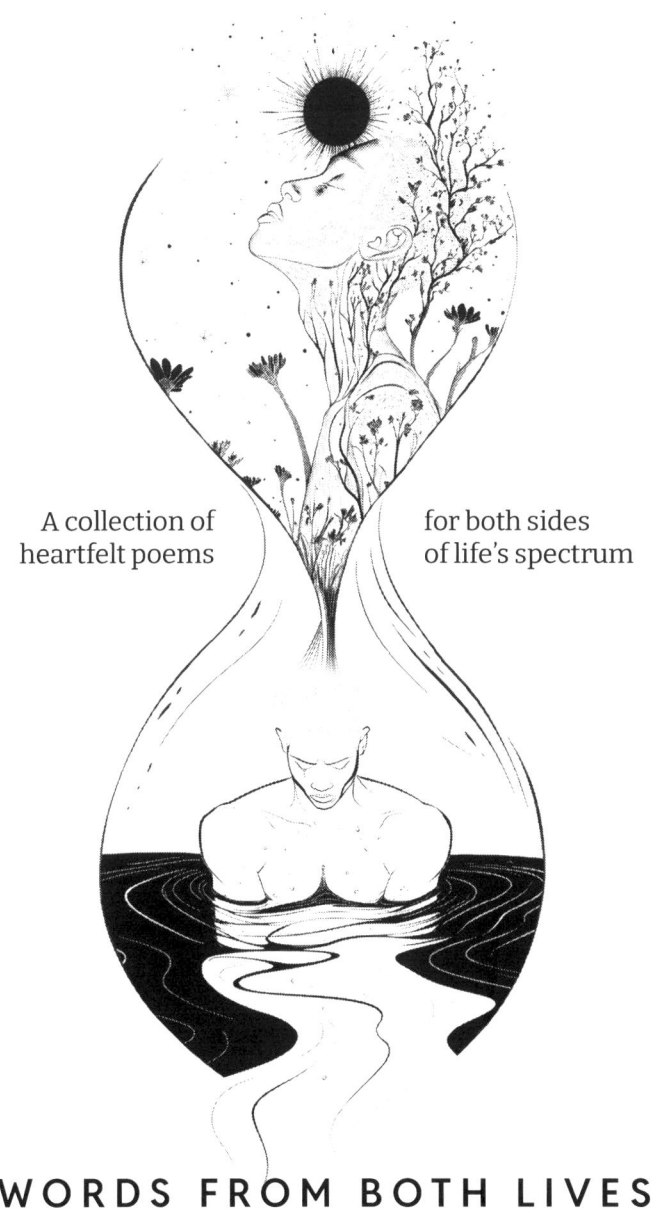

A collection of
heartfelt poems

for both sides
of life's spectrum

WORDS FROM BOTH LIVES

Copyright © 2024 by Ricco Francis

All rights reserved.
No part of this book may be used or reproduced in any manner whatsoever without the author's prior written permission, except for review uses permitted by copyright law.

Cover, interior and illustration design by Agata Filipczak (Niokoba)

A collection of heartfelt
poems for both sides
of life's spectrum

In loving memory of
Portland and Cheryl Francis

*In dedication to those
Without a voice to be heard*

CONTENT

Pain and love 13

WORDS OF PAIN 15

LOVE OF A PERSON 16
Seeing you with someone else 17
Thought of you 18
Only if I was good enough for you 19
I miss talking with you 20
The forgotten thought about you 21
Waited too long 22
Let's talk 23
Got no patience 24
Chess 25
Fishing line 26
Mind games on a good heart 27
Conspiracy 28
Conflict between two 29
Blocked 30

PERSONAL BAD LOVE 32
Love so hard 33
Unkind love 34
My guarded wall 35

OVERTHINKING / THOUGHTS 36
Lost sight 37
Obsessed 38
Addiction 39
Clouds 40
Ocean 41
Uncontrolled 42
Overload 43
View of judgement 44

A LOST PERSON'S SOUL — 46
Lied to myself — 47
Deeply broken — 48
I'm not enough — 49
Alone — 50
Sounds of lonely night — 51
Shy — 52
Lost voice — 53
False Image — 54
Self-harm — 55
Alcohol — 56
Grief — 57
Dying candles — 58
Understanding one's pain — 59
Depression — 60

MIS/COMMUNICATION — 62
Words unfelt — 63
Person, I hurt — 64
Mess-ups — 65
I lost a friend — 66
Helpers lost — 67
Betrayal — 68
The giver's gift — 69
Inconsiderate — 70
Hearts feelings — 71

UNFORTUNATE EVENTS — 72
Homeless — 73
Climate — 74
All good people die — 75
Nightmare hospital — 76
Cancer cruelty — 77
A loss — 79

IDENTITY CRISIS — 80
He — 81
She — 82

Becoming better half-heartedly 83
What it means to be black 84

UNNECESSARY USE OF POWER **86**
My dear, poor country neighbours 87
London youth 88
Evil within 89
War on my home 90
Vulnerable people 91
Bullies 92
Abusive power 93
Unconcerned wars 94

PRESSURE FROM THE WORLD **96**
Out of time 97
Wasted potential 98
Pressure 99

QUESTIONING **100**
Immortality 101
If love? 102
Stars 103
Sun 104

THE BRIDGES BETWEEN PAIN AND LOVE – PERSPECTIVE VIEWPOINTS: 107

Windows 108
Rose 109
Scales 110
Crows and doves 111

WORDS OF LOVE 115

LOVE OF A PERSON **116**
I got you 117
Idea of love 118

Person in front of you	119
My heart is yours	120
Old couple	121
About you	122
Care	123
Adjectives of love	124
True love's partner	125
The day I fall in love	126
Flower seeds of love	127
An unexpected rose	128
The one	129
For you	130
Universe	131
Patient-guarded walls	132
Those blue eyes	133
Deep blue eyes	134

APPRECIATIVE OF OTHERS — 136

Thankful for you	137
You Showed me	138
Helpers' voices	139
Stranger, I bumped into	140
Second chance	141
Dealing with conflict	142
Family and Friends	143
Kiss	144
Heart Beats	145
A young heart grew	146
Not truly gone	147
Animal Therapy	148
Auntie	149
Grandma	151

REINSURANCE OF SELF-LOVE — 154

Who you are	155
Stay calm	156
Simply breathe	157
I'm good enough	158
Don't come back	159

Value you 160
Mirrors 161
MY SOUL 162
When I was young 163
Ghost 164

HEALING AND HEALING FROM HURT **166**
Better days ahead 167
Music of happiness 168
Stories of overcoming struggles 169
My quiet place 170
Importance 171
I'm in control 172
Promise of tomorrow 173
Meditation 174
The senses of realisation 175
Perfume senses 176
Shower feelings 177
Home 178
Fight for 179
Change 180
Keep going 181

MOTIVATION AND LOOKING FORWARD **184**
Climbing mountains 185
Learning 186
Live freely 187
Happiest 188
New year 189
Life goals 190
Little Birds 191
Dance 192
Journey of a patient snail 193
Decision 194
My purpose 195

BRINGS YOU JOY AND IN LOVE WITH **196**
Midnight Drive 197
Rain 198

Light	199
Faith	200
Flowers	201
Story books	202
Chair	203
Dreams of the night	204
Travel Bugs	205
Rome	206
My favourite summer	207
Autumn	208
Walking through the park	209
I miss you, early 2000s	210
My love for the movies	211
Dis/Ability	212
Skin colours	213
Late night conversations	214
Your eyes	215
Everlasting time	216
Realisation you have love and happiness Afterall	217
Signs of art love	218
For my lost bright stars that need help	220
UK numbers	221
Dear Readers	223
Acknowledgements	225

Pain and love

Pain and love are different in many ways.
Felt from others more, or some feel it less.
However, they are both entwined by the contention
of emotional investment in something or someone;
It can be shown or felt in different forms, through issues
and themes, causing the pendulum to swing in any way
of experiencing love or pain at any threshold
but it should all be taken seriously, all the same.

WORDS OF PAIN

The signs of open wounds, loss,
dealing with pressure and anger

LOVE OF A PERSON

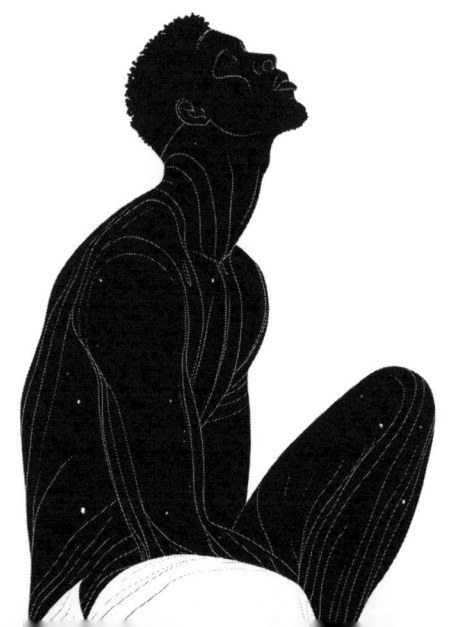

Seeing you with someone else

I hate the loss of function in my heart.
How it falters, stumbles
From seeing you are happy with another,
without a thought of me on your mind.

I still hold on,
hoping for a miracle,
of the memories we once shared
to pierce through your vision.

The thought of you laughing and smiling
at someone else's jokes, and not my own, hurts.
Leaving me broken,
the chaos that boils over my body,
my loss of control clouds over me entirely.

I hate that all my attempts to show you
I care about you, physically and emotionally,
meant nothing, as you moved on,
with no hesitation, no glance at what you left behind.

Even though I know I should move on,
and not choose to be blind,
the thought of you casually takes refuge in my mind,
in hopes of the greater grand scheme
sees you coming back in due time.

Thought of you

The thought of you every single day evokes suffering,
from the moment I wake up
to the moment I sleep,
you are the one constant thing I have visions of.

It is excruciating knowing
I'll never be able to be with you,
do the simplest things, like
hold your hands to bring you closer in,
see your smile when you're at your happiest,
bring you breakfast in the morning,
So, you never have to leave
the comfort of your bed.

I dream of messing around in the kitchen to our favourite songs,
laughing as life unfolds all around us.
But most of all, I wanted to know you better,
on a deeper layer, like
when an animal sheds its skin, revealing something
more beautiful beneath,

it's hard to breathe, knowing I'll never know you
the way I imagine you are.
Nights spent sitting in the darkness,
as hard-hitting hail drops echo my tears of loss.

I cling to hope,
hope of holding onto you,
even as endless anger brews within,
anger at the destined reasons we can't be together.

I hate that my thoughts can't quit
my declaration of my love for you forever.

Only if I was good enough for you

Only if I was good enough for you,
I would have seen the signs of the spiral of hurt
and been brave enough to act.
I wish I could be everything you need,
the one who keeps you going.

I'd be the air that you breathe,
the voice of calming melodies,
the grass that gently graces your feet
when you're alone outside, looking at the stars again,

I wish I could be your own personal clown
to make you laugh hysterically,
to bring joy where there's pain.
I wish I could be someone you loved forever,
The one you turn to when you have been hurt tremendously.

But only if I was good enough for you,
I would have been brave enough to fight for you,
to let you see the truth about how you make me feel.
I wouldn't have been this person—
scared of my own self-instincts,
unable to stand up for what my heart burns for.

I love the idea of your existence.
My heart burns with agony of not being with you.
My eyes start to leak when I think about you.
My soul feels hollow because
I'm not good enough for you.

Damaged by my own stupidity,
confidence lost in the trauma of my life before,
I've become quieter, like the sound of a pin drop—
barely there, never enough to hold you tight nonstop.

I miss talking with you

I miss talking with you.
You got me through my tough days,
not knowing if I was going to see another daylight.
The way you spoke so softly,
so calm and caring, like a swan in a lake.

I used to feel at ease with the words you said,
something so small of you telling me about the food that you ate.
The things that bring joy to your heart,
that makes you smile throughout your life,
the stories that are close to you, never to be forgotten.

I miss knowing if you're still okay,
because you made me
break the chains of depression,
the thoughts of self-blame,
the doubts of my existence,
the constant cycle of self-hatred.

I miss the long conversations,
with twists and turns of endless possibilities,
talking through the long hours of the night,
lost in this bubble of time,
only to be ended by our alarm clocks.

I miss the person who made me feel alive again,
by jolting my soul with everything that they are.
I hope to talk to you soon, in this life or the next,
to reminisce about the things that we did.

I miss talking with you.

The forgotten thought about you

Do you remember me?
The countless hours spent laughing by your side,
through the dumb jokes that weren't even funny
but meant everything to us.

The adventures of going out to places for the very first time,
only to get in trouble.
When you used to call me on your phone,
about something bad that's gone wrong,
I'll be at your front door in less than an hour,
to comfort you in kind songs.

My secrets were your secrets too and vice versa.
I was the key to unlock the vulnerable side of you.
Memories of you sharing out your dreams
were liberating to hear,
my dimples created a dent in my cheeks for my smile to appear.

Do you remember me now?
That I've disappeared from your life,
the days I thought about you,
you were busy forgetting.

I lost most nights to you,
through the old music we
used to listen to,
still hearing your voice
echo through my headphones.

I was the forgotten person in the years to come,
from the person I knew dearly.

Waited too long

I saw the girl my heart melted for,
climbed over hills to get her attention,
fell so deeply in love with everything that she was.
Her voice, that of a peaceful soul,
the smile of joy, like sunflowers on a sunny day,
her eyes were imbued with radiant moonlight shine.

Inside, she was more
than just a beautiful woman.
I so wish my conscience wouldn't have let me
play myself like a fool.
Now in the arms of another, warmth from their body aura,
she is lost in their eyes,
hypnotised by their love language,
and forgotten by their past lovers.

In torture, watching you happy with another,
In agony watching you kiss another,
I'm in torment, looking at the things
you and I were supposed to do,
but is done with someone new.

Only if I had the courage to ask,
we would be together—
but time ran out of the hourglass.

Let's talk

I hear your pain in many ways,
through the stories of heartache.
I learned about the hurt I've caused,
through the spiteful words that left you torn.
I damaged you emotionally,
thank you, as you have given voice to the other more hidden side of you.

I know I've hurt you emotionally,
I've been hurt by you too.
Through arguments, we left unsettled,
the ambush hits across our damaged hearts.

Let's communicate to acknowledge the grief,
the words we wish
we could take back,
by the Expressive tones we unleashed,
blindly Listening to each other's point of view,
In time, we thought we would heal from this trauma bruise.

Let's talk about forgiveness from the discussions,
the love we once shared with each other.
Our forced missing smiles when we were inseparable,
words of false love promises will come to light—
that you and I will always be close together,
but unfortunately, this was an example of a couple's toxic love lie.

Got no patience

Ain't got no patience,
always think I'm cheating,
never explained it to you,
no reason for me to change to be new.
When I say, baby, I love you,
I mean it.
I mean it!

Chess

Life is like a game of chess.
One wrong move, and your life is a mess.
Taking turns to hurt one's self-worth,
by knocking them off their pedestals.

Kings, queens, and knights in their own rights
are taking hits across the board
of emotional thoughts.
Arguments are going back and forth,
cornered with questions by rooks and pawns,
I lost my position due to my falling wall.

Bishops used to avoid straight questions,
Halfway down to take the queen's protection.
Pawns of great furious aggression,
one last move to take possession.
The board fell without answered questions,
falling piece of heartbroken tension.

Relief from our pain of endless moves,
restart the game they don't want to lose.
Chess forever wins.

Fishing line

Every day, my thoughts go back to you.
You're the fishing rod,
that makes me the fish.
I try to pull away,
but your grip on my thoughts.
My heart,
is too strong to let go.

Your strings lead to me
falling for the bait too many times.
You control which way we go,
up into the net you call home,
or, as I call it, a prison cell.
I'd rather be down there, free to escape,
from the grip of misleading promises, you make.

Free my young fish,
as there's more in the sea.
I hope the right one
eventually chooses me.

Mind games on a good heart

Which game was chosen today?
Playing on their heart strings,
toying with their minds,
draining the soul out of them,
a 'puppeteer master,' the best way to describe you.

Innocent by standards
was an object for your own
amusement,
by your own laughter.
Repercussions never
once fazed you.

Good hearts
belong to
those who brought
peace to them.
Unfortunately,
it leads to you.

Conspiracy

It was always me and you
until something changed within you.
You know I love you in every way;
don't make ten years just evaporate.

I've been there to get you through your therapy,
So don't come here with your conspiracy.
Because I can't look at you the same,
I can't just keep pretending I'm okay
when you can't trust the words, I say.

I thought this was more than an ordinary day,
so why did you act this way?
You have my heart,
don't let this break us apart.

High ocean wave alerts from far,
don't make this relationship unstable,
else I will have to jump overboard.
I think about the ship we were on,
I think we took the wrong course.

Because of your conspiracy
you lost all credibility
with your faith in me.

Conflict between two

The war goes on for months,
blowing words in each direction,
hitting shots like a rally of tennis,
only to be hurt when a compelling, valid score
of information is given.

The shaking of the room is echoing,
outbursts of bellowing arrows of pain
in the direction of the offence.
Is the law of strategic importance
to oversee the arguments
against you?

As trials go on for days,
the closed wounds from both sides
emerge open through the exchange of words
meant to dig so deep into their skins,
with the venomous words you used to say.
A wild animal you came to be,
a lover became a predator,
a carer became a predator.

Blocked

Loss of communication,
unresolved issues with turmoil,
a wall of silence,
guarded gates.

Blocked for reasons that were unknown,
lack of talking skills or acknowledgement,
paranoia and instant regrets,
insecurities from my lover's phone.

Jump to conclusions without a call,
I lost a person from my phone.
am I not good enough to perch on their soul?
Blocked by surprises with no warning lights.

Am I not good enough to bypass the gates
to enter their lives?

PERSONAL BAD LOVE

Love so hard

I love so hard that it ends up hurting.
The pain of real love,
the one I've been chasing,
ends up with more scars.

Countless tearful nights,
a featherless white bird
on a land isolated,
overthinking of my produced love.

Collapsing chemistry wires of the hearts,
wander through life's stages of healing,
only to be played again by cupid's
passionate desire of false love.

Unkind love

Love is unkind to those who love the most—
the hopeless romantics,
the caring bunch,
the ones who wait for those who don't.

Love is cloaked for so many.
Alone, sitting at home, staring out the windows,
thinking of their significant other.
Years have passed, and more are to come.

Countless rejections and regrets,
crying on the pillows, wet marks resonate within them.
Empty boxes of chocolates to fill up souls.
Love was never made for plenty hearts.

My guarded wall

A little noise echos through,
pale, dried colours
stain mood swings,
uneven marks across my broken heart.

Rock-solid metal,
bulletproof Steel,
a frame so strong,
protected like the Mona Lisa.

I won't break down,
for My foundations are entwined
by the emotional damages of my past.
My guarded wall is for those
who try to trespass into my complex,
uncontrollable loving heart.

OVERTHINKING / THOUGHTS

Lost sight

I fell so deeply in love with the idea of you,
the personality of you.
I put everything into my strength and energy
to show you how much I cared.

But I got lost in sight of the reason for loving you,
rushing thoughts of confusion,
trapped in my own head.
I said goodbye to my soul,
floating on to find a better life.

Here now stands an empty shell,
controlled by another.

Obsessed

Obsession is the weight of an anchor.
It dives so deep.
I see the light slowly dimming,
bouncing off the layer of blue sea,
leisurely drifting into madness.

I constantly have them moving in and round my brain,
from my very first thought in the morning
to entering my imagination during the day,
from minutes to hours.
A year lost in thoughts of you,
my dear obsession.

I wonder what you're doing now or even later.
I dream only of you,
in hopes it becomes reality.
My eyes are blinded by your mesmerizing beauty,
plus, the need of your persistent attention.

I'm a lost cause, drowning further,
without any warning or caution.

Addiction

Lost in a house of mirrors, with no exit in sight,
once a promise made to oneself, Turned into endless lies.
A cycle repeated from 1a.m back to the stroke of midnight.

The following enemies lurk in shadows,
whispering, ,'Do it again," for your light tunnel has vanished.

I have conversations with myself,
weighing out the pros and cons,
but deep down, subconsciously,
I already knew the right answer,
yet continue to proceed down
the rabbit hole of hurting my self-esteem.

Only for the short moment of enjoyment;
that is my darkest secret
I keep away from people's eyes.

The moment is over,
change in mind as guilt weighs over me.
I cried so much. I cried to the skies above
for nothing to return,
to soothe my ears in healing words.

The tunnel of light would always gradually appear,
until the enemies that lurk in the shadows
drag me in again, vanquishing the light as it disappears,
for I am lost within this house of mirrors' maze fear.

Clouds

Stormy nights take over,
take cover under my umbrella full of holes.
I lose sight of my own being.

Dark, rainy days with only the sights of
midnight streetlights along the edge of town.
I get lost in my own city of clouds,
visions of mist, and nowhere to go
but hearing rushing thoughts of unresolved problems.

As lightning strikes down on the clouds above my head,
I sense the judgement upon me.
The endless appearance of anxiety clouds.

Ocean

Oceans and waves of emotions
is the ship of loneliness.
Drifting through the tides of life,
I see an endless ocean line.

Tsunamis morphing into barriers,
I never want to reach land.

Uncontrolled

I hate that I overthink
and can't control the direction
of what lies ahead of my unfinished story.

Overload

Information gained so rapidly,
brain freezes on that very thought.
Memory stick overheated by
all the questions injected into your
cortexes of overwhelming emotions.

Unstable I stood,
grabbing onto something
strong to hold me up,
before becoming paralysed by
my own analysis of my life.

Boxed up and tightly packed,
came all the voices—
the voices that played
so roughly, in and around
my disconnected head.

View of judgement

I feel judgment on me
without any words or discussion
of who I am, or how I feel.
Am I not worth the time
or the care of someone's ear?

A LOST PERSON'S SOUL

Lied to myself

'Okay' was said on multiple occasions.
Self-belief was proclaimed.
You told yourself "I'm happy,"
the constant smiles
hurt your cheeks.

The holding back of tears
was a game for itself but
was ultimately upheld by you.
Your life quickly started to change
into an acting role.

You forgot the way to
ask for help.
From that moment on
I knew I'd lied to myself.

Deeply broken

Fragile tender hearts and broken dreams,
those dear memories dissolved.
A family I wished would believe in me,
I see someone living out my dreams of acting out those movie scenes.

As the rain pours, I hear the loneliness of countless tired tears.
What could have been is not what is now,
for not living out your dreams.
Frustration and anger at yourself.
Scars and bruises across your cheeks
which once was used to smile.

I tell myself it will be okay,
but nothing seems to really change.
It's not like the weather is one day warm and one day cold.
It's more like a black hole, colourless, just like my soul,
and I hope one day it will change.

When I find my purpose
I hope I will feel whole again.
At this moment, I just feel broken.

I'm not enough

The reflection I see in front of me
is one of disappointment.
For they have no identity in who they are.
Cracks and fragments across the mirrors
of souls escaping from their
dark-hosted bodies,
only to be found in someone more suited.

I hate every inch of myself,
for I am the disease that haunts so many others.
The plague that causes so many deaths in my presence,
which is not supposed to exist.

I'm not safe to be around.
I'm not the light that uplifts the world,
but the owner who holds the chains,
sending us back into darkness.
Furthermore, I wish I was good enough for people to be in my life,
but I'm the cause of so much sadness, hurt, and pain.
I am the forgotten creature of the hell pits' fire flames.

Alone

Being alone is like a void,
where you try to climb out from
but is never-ending.
No matter how hard you climb.

Sounds of silence all around.
In space, drifting on to an even darker place,
shadows are soon to take over.

There was no light to be seen in the distance,
no sounds of
any assistance from loved ones to friends,
who don't really see as
their torch ran out of batteries.

I'm completely stranded on my own island.

Sounds of lonely night

Echos of sad stories linger overnight.
The empty shelves, which were once filled with love letters envelopes,
are covered in dusty cobwebs.

The giant rooms, which once were full,
are now a place of memories,
ones to reminisce about the times of shiny skies.

A big heart mended through time,
a needle of blood bounded with the emotional losses of
the loved ones in the afterlife.

The vinyl records I'll listen to
keeps the mind in harmony.
Next door's noises make me smile.

I'm not so alone or empty.
The surrounding sounds are
my personal company—
ones deep within the shadows.

Shy

Voice on mute,
sweat along my face,
I lost the way to talk about past pain.
the way to express how I feel to others—
words aren't enough for me anymore.

I keep quiet when I'm around you,
close my eyes to not see you,
head down to forget you.

Nervous handshakes meet people full of energy.
I once had it, but it has been lost for eternity.
The weirdest perplexed smile crosses my face
when people want to know me.

In my closet, hidden,
please don't save me.

Lost voice

The ability to speak freely was gone
from past trauma.
My vocal cords modified so drastically,
so robotic with low-frequency sounds,
muttered out of my mouth, unrecognisable
of how it used to be.

Staring into my mirror,
practicing my words in a sentence uncomfortably,
I choked on the words pronounced by me,
clawing at my throat in
hopes it will fix my anxiety.

I miss the loud bass drums
the high note keys,
the ability for someone to hear me from
across the street.

My voice was lost through the things
that I've been through in my history.

False Image

Alone, dealing with the problems and stresses,
I cry endless tears like rivers flow each night
when I'm alone again.

Room-flooded floors,
punch marks engraved on walls—
this is my real image.

Putting down my mirrors when I'm alone
so, no one can bear witness.

Fake smiles and fake laughs when with people
to hide how I'm really feeling,
but deep Down hoping they find the cracks
within my false image, but they never do.

I hide them from others because I don't want them to worry—
an emotion mask I've placed on my face.
Day to day, to hide underneath my real Identity,
of unbearable pain.

Self-harm

Not born with hatred for one's own self,
I have not prophesied to hate every inch of my body.
Loved by others, but not by me,
my existence is what I want to burn out completely.

Years of anger, Years of self-doubt,
years of self-blame along with guiltiness
of things, I never caused initially—
lost the battle from within myself.

Scars, in addition to bruises,
were left across my body:
my arms, my legs,
the cheeks that were once used to quirk a smile.

Sharp objects were used to inflict physical pain—
I was the reason for the action to take place.
A sense of temporary relief Came urging on,
long jumper sleeves to cover arms, hands inside of them to cover fingers,
turtlenecks to cover my neck, long trousers to cover the legs.

This was only worn in the presence of others,
a cloak of invisibility to hide the shame of
uncontrollable, unstable Emotions
which took reign.

Tomorrow is the same;
a blade is being used
to temporarily take
the pain away.

Alcohol

Every night, I use alcohol
to drink all problems away,
push down the thoughts of any solutions,
the magic potion that hypnotises the mind,
forgetting any feelings.

Alcohol was the substance for pain relief,
the painkiller tool used to flush down deeper
anger, loneliness, and the cry for help,
lost at the bottom of the reusable bottle.

Sickness overwhelmed me,
morning headaches were Irresistible,
chest aches were unmeasurable,
liver failure was imminent.

This didn't sway the outcome,
as the benefits of alcohol
consumed my judgement
causing me to lose myself
completely in this cycle.

Grief

No thoughts on crying, at any points of time,
It happens so naturally, it's no point of trying.
As For the heart break,
In that memory,
you're still processing in real time.

Body is shaken Through the loss of a person I knew,
from birth and to adulthood,
looking through
the photos of old, memories Came
rushing back.

The texts messages, I still look through,
seeing the plans we made, but you never kept them,
because you were gone too soon,
leaving me here, alone to try hard
to move on with the Metaphoric broom.

Doing things to Keep my mind off you,
my hobbies grew,
but so, did
the thoughts of you.

Only time will tell,
and when teardrops Settle,
I will finally accept and say,
goodbye to you.

Dying candles

The artificial lights of my dreams
are slowly evaporating.

with every enlightening dream of mine,
the wax starts melting over my head.

Covering the thoughts of my self-awareness,
the forever calmness becomes unstable.

As I go beneath the layer of my bathtub,
surrounded by the candles that once brought-

a scented piece of luxurious warmth, now intoxicated
by the eternal, dying flame of rushing burns from my past mistakes.

I lost the race of reducing my stress from the candles
that once stood tall but are now nowhere to be seen again.

Those candles died on me,
leaving me
in darkness.

Understanding one's pain

I heard the news that I've heard once before;
one of pain and sorrow.
The darkest memories returned from a distant place.
I saw the look in their eyes, eyes that used to belong to me.

Fake smiles to those who tried to comfort us,
but underneath a pile of dirt is the buried
screams of constant hurt,
which we want the air to feel,
but only behind closed doors.

Younger than me, those people were
when they lost their very world,
a person so meaningful,
their presence will be missed,
from the dining table,
when they have a family meal.

My heart aches for those two
important people. As the very things
you used to do with that special person
are now even harder to accomplish.

Depression

Looking for light, but there are no exit signs,
despite holding on to the smallest bit of happiness,
you're never truly happy.
Depths of trepidation thoughts slowly creeping in,
holds down any hopes of feeling better again.

Countless days in your bed, a lifeless
casket laid, no point of moving on.
There's no place to go.

Growth-wise,
it was not made for me.
At some point, I stopped the cries.
Because I had no use for them anymore.

No remote for facial expressions;
for my face, it was a blank canvas.
Emptiness was the perfect word to describe me,
pain was excruciating
to relay.

MIS/COMMUNICATION

Words unfelt

The unleashing of feelings
was a beacon sign—
outcalls and cries
lasted continuously.

Emotional speeches,
held from 10pm
to 3am in the morning.

The tug of your shoulders
was a gesture of my needed help.

Blind-eyed, they chose to be,
changing the subject of
The clear message.

My dear people,
defined by obliviousness.

The words spoken were silent
lost in a bubble
never to be released.

Feeling of a Lifetime
of irrelevancy.
words were never
a use for me.

Person, I hurt

The person I hurt so many times,
you kept coming back to me.
Through the times apart,
forgiveness was a trait of yours.

As for mine, it was constantly hurting you.
How hard I tried to stop my crimes,
for making you cry.

The love I gave was uncontrollable,
I loved even harder.
I was blinded by your needs,
a failing relationship
came crashing down.

Through my actions,
I damaged the person
I never intended
on hurting—
the person
that deserved
better than me.

Mess-ups

No matter how much I try, I mess everything up.
I try to uplift my friends, but with the wrong advice.
Messing up is a birth right of mine—
mine alone.

So close to getting over the hurdles,
only to fall so short.
I want to clean up all the mistakes I've made,
the stains across the brains of other's pains.

Conundrums get me into trouble,
too much pressure on fixing patches,
it burst their bubbles.
Uncleared, I made it be.

I lost a friend

I lost a friend,
the Person who gave me comfort
When I had my own worries.

They would hug me like a Sponge,
to squeeze the excess problems out.
Hurt of my own self-doing,
for it was the crime

I committed in front of them
belittling their kind heart into a corner,
to make them feel sorry for me,
in hopes that they would never leave.

A sort of dog collar was chained
along their lifeline, owned by me.
Friendship changes to cruelty,
love changed to over obsession.

A person who used to see
me as someone
now only saw the shadows
of my toxicity.

Helpers lost

Your positive energy always gets drained
by those who use it.
But are they never there when you need refilling?

I gave them hugs.
I gave them kisses.
Not only that, but I gave them words of reassurance.

"You don't need to know your self-value.
I see how much you are worth."

From that day on, I saw a caterpillar
change into a butterfly, so beautiful and strong.
It flapped its wings' goodbye,

leaving its helper grounded in emotions,
shattered down with no energy,
hoping to be released from their own cocoon.

Betrayal

I told someone my deepest secrets
in hopes they'd keep them.
In time, those secrets
slowly crept out from a hidden
Treasure chest.

The golden messages
soon to be shared for all those other ears.

Something so valuable becomes so worthless.
My trust in that person died at that very moment.
I hear the very things I tried to bury
underneath my forgotten memories,

resurfaced by another person's lips.
The trojan horse to enter in with full trust
was full inside with distrust and lies.

Loyalty was lost that day,
for my heart was left wide open
for the betrayal arrow
to hit me where I stood.

The giver's gift

Never to receive,
only to be used
for those whose faces of true
intentions are hidden away

Behind the curtain, like a certain wizard
of deceptive promises.

The giver's heart is laced in gold and purity,
only to be shared
with others,
for their hands
are reached out
in true need, help.

Too blind-sighted
the giver was traded
with dirt for gold,
with pollution
for purity,
leaving the giver empty.

Inconsiderate

Those ears were made for listening,
most people are accustomed with the knowledge to.

Sounds of paroxysm,
processed and gathered by the
thoughts of others were accepted into
words of forgiveness.

There are very few who are not familiar
with whispers placed within their ears of narcissism,
by no sense of direction into feeling wrong.

Empathy and sympathy, they had no insight in,
blinded by their own ignorance because
they are always right.

It's hard to reason with those without a doubt.
A fight breaking out
when they are accused of
the wrongdoing.

Hearts feelings

Our hearts are literally caged.
Maybe that is why
it's so hard to say
how we really feel inside.

UNFORTUNATE EVENTS

Homeless

Cold, rainy nights across the whole country
while we warm up near our fireplace and drink hot chocolate,
in the house of warmth,
there is another place open to
the harsh conditions of Mother Nature.

Many did not choose their fate,
of sleeping in the winter nights in
the streets of London,
praying to survive overnight in hopes
to see the dawn of day once again.

Food shortages every time,
the fights with the other discarded people
for the scraps of less-regarded foods we leave behind.
the homeless people
are the voices of pleading noises we hear at night,
for their screams and cries
is about the reminiscence of their early bright lives.

The sad stories echo for thousands of years
through every street corner
and every crack of your cosy place you call home.
They are the lost ones,
who float along
hoping to be brought back to shore.

Climate

I do wonder how long the earth will continue
to become hotter than its predecessor.
Swinging axes to cut down trees in the forests,
In order not to breathe—
doesn't make sense to me.

Carbon dioxide
plus, the major greenhouse gases
are killers agents?
forests are home to many species, but we are the executioners.

We shouldn't be the hierarchy nor be obedient to authority.
However, the guardians of peace
fossil fuels are too heavily relied upon. For their properties
catastrophe struck, by our inability to see.

We are burning our very own world apart,
wildfires and extreme weather events
across land and seas,
increased risks of diseases
to land degradation.

Awaken our eyes to the erupting
devastation
of our planet
Earth.

All good people die

I thought I knew about the world, but I misunderstood.
Why do all the good people die?
With all the bad things, still surviving,
why do we let this define us today?

Because all the good people,
they die without getting a choice in life.
I see how the world was supposed to work, but it seems
you can't ever do anything right.

Why in hell did we survive?
I wish I could trade my life
for the fallen innocent lives.
The world has changed from what it was meant to be;
stabbings, shootings and unfortunate accidents are
not supposed to be the norm to me.

Fighting over things which are so unnecessary;
we're supposed to be living in Harmony
Fixing the world and helping out,
showing love by doing the right things.
This is what good people do, but all the good people die.

They are cure for most diseases, but some
are the unlucky ones,
from unfortunate events,
which led to black attire
and speeches from loved ones.

Good people get cursed, young or old,
we can't save them all,
that's the part that really hurts.
The justice scales have been
heavily unfavoured.

Nightmare hospital

A place that haunts me in my dreams,
in reality, it's even more terrifying.
My chariot awaits to bring me back
to this place of nightmares.

Flashing lights across my chariot
to tell others to make way,
it's almost time for the passenger
to meet their fate.

Rushed inside this place that save lives,
unfortunately for the passenger's family,
it was not possible this time.
Hours were spent duelling
with the Fatal conditions,

The passenger's family waited,
in screams and cries,
thoughts of uncertainty
played on repeat,

until the moment of death
it became revealed to them.
Pain lasts even longer than before.
Another life buried by the cursed family of mine.

The hospital became
a haunted house for me,
as this was a journey cycle
that my family and I could never escape from.

A bond shared by death,
agreements shared by blood,
a loss of a family member
it took place inside the hospital bed.

Cancer cruelty

It's dormant in all of us
only some are selected,
unexpectedly surprised
by an unwanted gift
that springs forth
like a Jack-in-the-Box.

It latches to our lifeline,
a symbiotic, parasite that
feast on our cells—
the cells that once produce
the love inside of us.

Cancer is the word we fear.
It lingers in our brains,
a dark cloud we try to make disappear,
but is tightly attached
to our subconscious minds.

Doctor visits and checkups,
moments of clarity
only for some, as others are
brought with the news of the thing
we fear
to Reappear within their ears.

Cancer affects so many,
the silent invader
that sinks its venomous teeth internally,
but yet finds a way to somehow escape
to haunt the loved ones externally—
the ones who watch to see the changes
of the targeted, unfortunate ones.

Deteriorating in health, deteriorating in emotion,
I witnessed the person I loved
given up persevering—
from optimism to despair.

Despite the chemotherapy working,
the visible side-effects were clear:
loss of hair, fatigue, nausea and vomiting
And the constant pain of misery.

As days passed, I often see
my loved one become more sickened
by the catastrophe, which is cancer.
I prayed and hoped for their recovery,
to return to the days of joyful memories.

But as darkness took over and the consumption
was done,
I lost my very world to cancer,
as their heartbeat was gone.

A loss

A loss is a loss, no matter who you are,
painful experiences shared across to the stars.
Light is shone over, for all of us to glance,
a loss is a loss,
that takes on different forms, perchance.

Huge or miniature,
it leads to stitches,
across our
Journey
paths.

IDENTITY CRISIS

He

He's cursed by the perspective of
modern day Masculinity.
Kings of high-end riches they must be,
not the state of sustainability,
for it is not good enough.

Pressure from the social society,
in Messages for how to be the ideal man.
Body shapes and wealthiness are all classified,
not hearts of gold nor good intentions, for they
are all blocked from entering
our unrealistic Expectations.

It's shameful to see how males
never uplift each other.
Hidden in plain sight,
crying out their feelings
as in the open world
it makes you less of a man.

I've lost all hope on what
it is like to call myself
a true man.

She

In a box due to a mixed society,
being pretty is a gift and a curse.
A perfect woman doesn't exist,
no matter how much we try.

"Must look beautiful"
is the top priority? But the hypocrisy,
when people say,
"You are nothing more than a pretty face."
A classic line they always say—
"one wet wipe can take that away."

For those who don't have that luxury,
pressure on your shoulders for having
your own independence, but once again,
society says a man wants you to stay in bed,
for the males will provide for you.

I'm like a rope for tug of war,
stuck in the middle of these constant thoughts.
Which way am I supposed to go
when being a woman has still
not been defined today
by the society of pressured
disagreements between us as the
human race?

Becoming better half-heartedly

Expecting to strive to become someone better,
but not changing who you currently are,
with the utmost respectful regards,
this is a true remark of irony.

First, you've got to love yourself entirely
before
uttering a half-hearted statement
for all of us to laugh out,
in hysterical entertainment.

What it means to be black

I didn't choose to be this colour,
your skin is different and more superior.
My skin is darker, my skin is in pain,
my skin is shouting out to be saved.
aren't we supposed to be the same?

Because you don't know what it's like to be black—
broken souls, smashed bodies,
and crushed voices which have been stolen from us
from all those centuries ago.

Narratives have been picture-framed by the smallest
minority groups of our cultural roots,
but that doesn't mean all of us are the same
as those who cause harm to you.

A war on us is a war on you,
for remember,
we are all the same species, in truth,
you must look deeper than what just stands
in front of you.

UNNECESSARY USE OF POWER

My dear, poor country neighbours

Blinded by the news coverage
of my fellow citizens across
the other side of the world,
false images and tales painted
of their culture's heritage.

They're hurting people
who have suffered from world-wide disasters,
such as food shortages,
medicine scarcity,
the lack of shelter and the inability
to escape wars easily.

There is so much more
that people are blinded to see.
We are lost in our thoughts,
of main character energy.
The lessons learned from
our previous lives as adolescence
have been forgotten.

The lesson of caring more than
the family and friends
that stand in front of you,
but the other people who live with you on
this earth we call home.

So be more considerate,
and have more gratitude,
as my dear poor country Neighbours
(may) suffer more than you.

London youth

Dear London youths, I know you're hurting,
born or chosen for wars
for nothing.
The loss of lives from pointless fighting,
I hate how many parents are out there crying
over their loss of their children.

I wish they opened their eyes
the lives they live should not be glamorised,
for it costs a fair amount
of bloodshed across our streets of London.

I know you once had ambitions
to become something greater than
the achievements of a life sentence.
Tied to your street code, in too deep,
no hopes of escape from the endless beef.

I know it's hard with beliefs
of no way out,
but trust me, there's more than one
route out of the streets.
Knives are tools of harm—
we need to place them down,
that's one life safe from a fearful fate.

Seek help from those around, for you will
surely escape.
dear London youths,
you have more to give to this world
then taking lives away.

Evil within

A crime committed against
the natural world order of law
that changes everything.
My awareness was now
altered by forces inside of me,
inflict damages to every
single part of me.

The pain that followed,
caused by my controlling
demons, hurt in every aspect.
The things I'll do are unthinkable,
the sins of man were preached
in joy, not in disgust.

I watched my control drift away.
What was despicable before
became good in the
eyes of a fallen, pure soul.
My demons locked
the goodness away
within me.

War on my home

The door with chains were broken into,
smashed-up windows, glass flying everywhere,
scattering across the floors
of my cozy home.

Hidden in plain sight, in hopes I was not found,
I've lost all hopes for duality.
Breathless, I came to be sweating unnaturally.
I remember the times when humans were friendly.

Safety cameras and the alarm system
now installed on my property
to protect myself
from the same species as me.

Untrusted visitors were here
to take what was mine.
To leave me without a resemblance of who I am.
I lost the very things I would call home.

Now, unfortunately, I welcome you
to what's left of my humble abode.

Vulnerable people

They are the most innocent
in expression and physicality.
gentleness was their speciality.
exploitation was beholden
upon them for their needed
expectation to deliver your
desired plans.

I am the voice for the voiceless,
as their voices have been silent
through the Destructive Abuse
by your hands.

Spread the word,
so that they can be heard,
in hopes of searches
promising their freedoms.

Bullies

Dear bullies,

You have the power to stop,
but you continuously cause me so much harm—
physically, emotionally, and mentally.
From your point of view, it makes you laugh,
but I don't know how that's even funny,
because you left me here with scars
inside and out of my body.

The cry to my parents to keep me home
because I'm horrified to be in your presence
when I'm alone inside the same building as you.
Why do you have so much animosity
towards me? is it because I'm smaller,
Less cool, or maybe it's because
I'm smarter and more driven than you?

Which I don't mean to say impolitely,
or is it that you have
Low self-esteem and your own personal problems,
So, you take your anger out on me?
It's not fair that you choose me or even anyone at all,
as my days are filled with torture and abuse.
but I was also met with quiet ears from others-
when I plead for help,
is my life less meaningful?

Because right now, I feel deeply miserable,
undesirable and inevitable to take now,
my last breath, so let this be a life lesson to check on everyone,
because you never know when or if their lives might be at threat.

To my bullies, I hope this made you understand.
We could have just been great friends
instead of pushing me off the edge of the cliff,
waiting for a hand to lift me up again.

Abusive power

Take advantage of those who are weaker,
you are nothing more than an abuser.
Knock them over and kick them around,
uncaring about the damage you leave behind.

All for power, all for growth,
I see how far you will go.
Hunger was your downfall,
blinded by your own greed.

Neglect all around you,
but you chose not to see.
Intolerance was the word meant for you.

Unconcerned wars

So much death, so many losses,
when I heard the news, saw the aftermath.
Not easy for those who are faint hearted,
only anger comes to thought.

So powerless were citizens of those war-torn countries,
vile, irrational actions committed by those in power.
No care or love for those affected,
devastating planned-out plots have now come into effect.

Living innocent lives have now turned to unplanned deaths.
It's hard to grasp how much we are the biggest threats
to our own planet, maybe we shouldn't have
been allowed out of the treasure chest of life.

When all we choose is the sharpest knife
to slaughter, which is the gift of living out a well
flourished, earnest life without the fearful thoughts of cruelty crimes.

PRESSURE FROM THE WORLD

Out of time

My dreams I once dreamt
are dying out.
The concept of having to live out
the idea of what I wanted my life to be
scars deeper into the tissues of hope.

Years spent dancing and singing
with the intention of there being
an outcome of stage performance,

led to years of ageing
with the promise of
The odyssey to still turn
the dream to reality.

I feel am out of time.
The pressures of the world,
opportunities slowly started
to close on me.

The dreamer of the night
began to creep into the
nightmares of failure.

Wasted potential

Life is something new with the
Potential to be more.

Life is not lived to the fullest.
Not free, not allowed with barriers
which holds us back.

When we truly want to be more,
by the idea of making life better,
an open space for our ambitions
to be sought out
indefinitely.

Pressure

I feel the weight of the world around me,
deep beneath hesitation is on me,
diminishing my dreams,
in this never-ending bottomless pit,
holding me back from reaching own life goals.

Hardly able to stop the panic attacks,
providing food, clothes and shelter,
paying bills for rent is incredibly difficult.

When they are raising prices up
my family looks at me
to provide
to survive.

I only wish the government
could see
the pressure is on
to barely live
in London city.

QUESTIONING

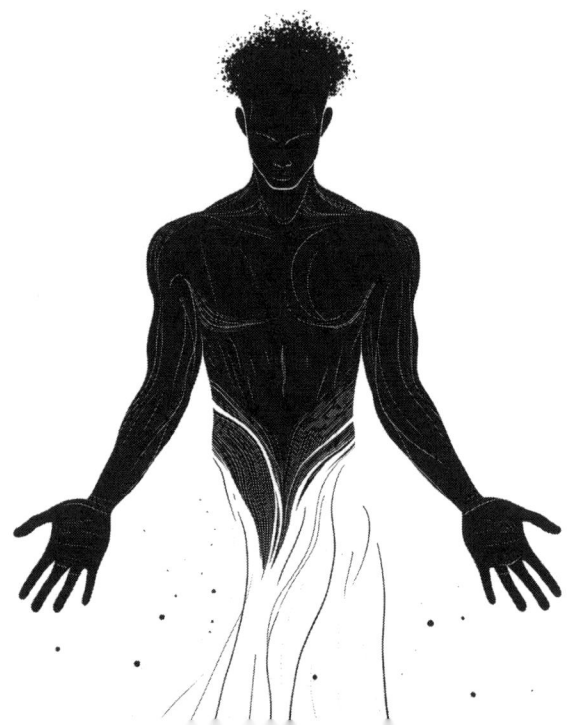

Immortality

Once was a gift?
With the oldest eyes,
wise knowledge kiss
internal loneliness.

Loved ones have passed.
the life cycle carries on,
eternal sunshine of hell.

I wished for many more years.
Then I could imagine
I saw discoveries and wonders.
Through life's lenses,
immortal I came to be.

Dark red rain fell from the sky.
From a dream to a nightmare,
graphic images bled through my eyes.
Horrors of generations,
immortal contrast of light and dark.

Death, I cheer for it to take me.
As I left this place,
I smiled graciously,
passing through the gates of heaven.

If love?

If love is so universal,
why haven't I found
my destined version
of devoted love?

Stars

If stars are meant to be seen from afar,
how will I ever get close to one?
(Stardust was potent in their eyes for they did not know it yet)

Sun

"You compare me to the sun,
as I might bring warmth,
but I can never get too close?"

("Warmth to my heart you provided me so,
but this is my voyage along the river water
where which the sun cannot go")

THE BRIDGES BETWEEN PAIN AND LOVE

PERSPECTIVE VIEWPOINTS:

Windows

Life is like a window;
we can see things from both sides vividly.

Rose

What does a rose signify:
love or poison?

How do you intend to use
this ambiguous symbol?

Scales

I lost the ability to think
through the whispers of others in my ears
and the sounds of serpent tongues,

clouding my self-judgment of the balance scales,
which were once weighted by the fruits of Eden.

Scales now unbalanced
by the immoral compass of unlucky interference.

My heart was Judged by Anubis,
the Egyptian guardian of scales,
to see if I was guaranteed safe passage
to the afterlife.

Crows and doves

Darkest crows and the brightest doves

Far apart but close in heart,

in Joint enterprise to show pain and love.

One brings peace and the other
comes with death.

Crows like shadows, cold and sharp,
Doves like light, warm and sweet to hold in me.

Crows squeak out in haunting tones
echoing fears, whispers of silent gravestones.

Doves hum songs of healing notes,
lifting hearts to where the sun goes.

Crows are scars we try to hide
from People's eyes
wounds that ache
yet still abide
by the actions to
our flight.

Doves are warmth in our tender hands
a strong sense of soothing charms
that heal the broken threads
that divides our hearts.

Yet both are part of who we are—
pain and love, near and far.

Crows and doves, in every breath,
shape our journey, life and death.

For in our hearts, both must reside,
the hurt we feel, the love inside.

Crows and doves will forever
remain entwined, in every
soul they both will find Refuge.

WORDS OF LOVE

The signs of healing, enjoyment, happiness,
affection and rediscovery

LOVE OF A PERSON

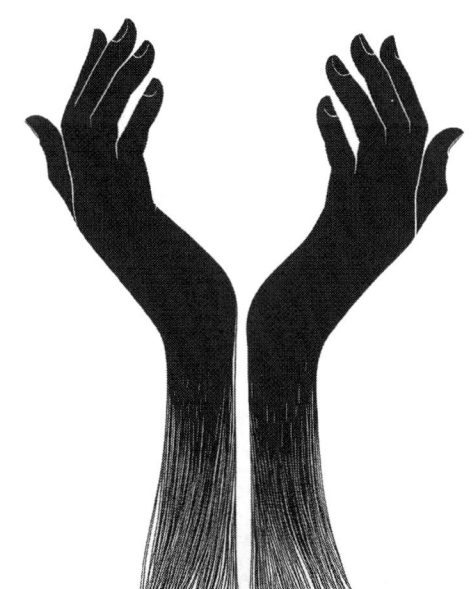

I got you

I've got you now and forever.

Use me like a support system,
never to malfunction.

I'm here to help you with anything.
I'm here to hold your hands in the cold,
to keep you warm, like the fireplace in the winter nights.

The mechanic to fix you when you break down
through the loss of internal thoughts,
the doctor to mend your funny bones
to see the smile, you once had return.

The photographer to capture the moments
of life you were so incredible proud of,
to placing them inside your own art galleries.

I've got you like a life jacket,
never to let you sink down into your own hole of shame,
but to uplift you into a place of peace.

I got you, like a baby needs a parent
who cares and loves them with every fibre of their existence.

I've got you forever.
I will always be there for you.

I've got you.

Idea of love

You are the spark in my heart.

To keep the hopes of lights on,
the love I so long for inside,
I can't stop believing in the idea of love.

When you're the embodiment of love,
your smile warms every molecule in my body.
Your touch is my safe place, not a cage, but a
home.

Your words are like a siren, not to lure me in,
but to hold me close.
Romance grows more with how much time I'm in your hands.

Love is the word
you gave meaning to.
I grace your love language.

Person in front of you

The person in front of me,
is the person I want to spend the rest of my life with indefinitely.

The person in front of me is the person I'm going to cherish for years to come.

The person in front of me is the one for whom I'm going to be there for,
in their highs and lows, no matter how much energy needed to be drained.

For it is not a sacrifice; for my heart will not sink low, merely
like a blood transfusion to spring the love within them alive again.

This person is someone who doesn't need to know yet,
you were so much more than just a person from the very first moment we met.

You are everything that is worth waking up for, fighting for, and
loving more.

You are everything that is good about the world. You are my medicine.

Furthermore, you make me a better person.

This person in front of me is someone
I'll care for without failure.

My heart is yours

My heart is yours.
When I say your name, my heart beats.
When I see your face, my heart beats.
When I see your eyes, my heart beats.
When I see you play with your hair, my heart beats.
When I see your laugh, my heart beats.
When I see your smile, my heart beats faster.

When I see you sad, my heart aches.
When I see you every day, my heart melts.

My heart is yours for eternity.
My heart beats for you.
My heart is there for you.
My heart will always love you.

My heart is yours.

Old couple

I glance through my bedroom window
to see this old married couple holding each other's hands,
bound by the love-told story of a millennium.

I wonder how many times
their love grows from all their previous lives,
the love I see in them
Is the love that I want to have.

They shared a beautiful relationship one of not-easy roads.
They are now in unison, Shaped by shared ups and downs,
overcome by the love they saw in each other's eyes
from the very first moment they met.

I want to have what they have,
years of discovery on your partner's
personality and their likes,
by contrast, what makes them feel sad and want to cry.

I know in this world; it was meant to be—
those two are forever now.
There is no doubt in their hearts content.

No matter if one dies,
their love will still be for them.

An old married couple
passed through my life
at the very right time.

About you

Months ago, I came across someone
I would lose track of time for.

Lose the ability
to comprehend as
I got lost in their eyes and
their smile.

The Dumbest thing
was getting lost in them,
I didn't know them well,
I just knew it was
the beginning of the journey
to getting to know them better.

Care

I'll care about you always.
I care so deeply that I hate how much I mess up.

I try so hard because I want to impress you,
that includes not to curse in front of you.
That makes me a chivalrous man.

I can't believe you exist,
because you're the embodiment of prioritising,
sharing your heart and your soul to someone-
even with chances for you to potentially plunge a dagger in my heart,
leaving a hole.

A person of truth,
I'll be audaciously honest rather than die lying.
I'm not afraid to tell you that you're affectionate, honest, and real.

I write because of you.
I care for you.

Adjectives of love

My Romance language
Is unmeasurable.

My words will never be enough,
like how my love for you
changes and grows.

However, I'll always use the adjectives of love
to let you know that you are loved.
Each day, I'll use them to describe
my feelings for you.
Each day after that,
I'll accumulate more powerful adjectives
to explain why it will always be you.

My adjectives of love are used to describe
my emotions, you make me feel,
The personality traits you give,
love actions committed by both of us.

Expressive Love through
the words of communication,
dans ma langue romane des adjectifs.

True love's partner

All these people that live among us,
but all I care about is you, only you.

I have endearment for you.
I see my past, present and future with you.
No one else will ever break the bond or the promises-
promises made to each other,
because I'm devoted to you by my indestructible contract,
signed by the blood that pumps my heart.

I love you, and when I die,
I'll remember you with the memories that will live forever,
even when I pass this life into the next.
I love you, my forever person.

The day I fall in love

The day I fall in love in this moment of time, an unbreakable window between you and me will open. You see me in every second, every minute, every hour, and every moment of my life, just as I did. The day I fall in love, the connection between two beings will be inevitable. A light that burns so strongly that the darkness fades away like the storms from the sky. You are the only one I see from inside and out of your body, your flesh, your soul, and everything that comes with you. I love you so much, beloved, in many ways, and there are so many metaphors I could use to describe the way you look and how you make me feel. I can't wait for that day to come so soon. When I finally meet you.

Flower seeds of love

Deep depths of rooted seeds
Implanted in your mated
soil, brain of chemistry.

Pollen of emotions,
uncontrollable outbursts
of raging beauty fumes.

The flower I want to be
is one with colour and
Empathy, a flower that
sways and dances in
the wind.

For I want to
stand out for the love
I have rooted deep within me.

I see the colours of
wonders across my eyes,
for your flower is more divine.

My seeds grow in hopes of
loving another
flower so beautiful,
a flower so strong,
a flower that wishes to grow with me.

An unexpected rose

Finding that right, perfect rose
in a bouquet is everything.
Even when it's unexpected,
it still has those beautiful qualities
to blossom.

The one

You were the one I put my guard down for,
the only one I shared a spark with,
the only person I felt so deep for.

Losing you will be the death of me.
You help get rid of my unwanted premonitions.

Deeper with love for you—
you are truly the one.

For you

It hurts how much you push me away,
but the thought of you brings me closer.

To look under the microscope of your personality,
the gift of your soul within you,
like a biography book flipping over the pages
of your life's big stories,
from a young age to adulthood.

Love and pain you faced internally,
with words unspoken through years
of untrusted Candidates for
lies and manipulation,
has closed your heart again.

For I see your lock and
I hope to be the key to set you free.
The thought of you is
the love I seek.

Universe

In a universe that keeps expanding,
with so many stars, planets, solar systems and galaxies,
Why do I only want to know you on this tiny planet we call Earth?
You're my own universe, a boundless realm which I seek to explore—
delving deeper into your mystery of the person I'm yet to fully see.

In the Japanese word of yugen,
a Profound beauty and depths that transcends the limitations of words.
Revealing an essence beyond expression.

Patient-guarded walls

Be patient with the one you love.
As they trusted hard in the past
and were left with crushed walls of lies.

So, it takes a long time
for them to slowly put down their walls again.
To let you in.

Be the healer of lies
by shining truthful light into their hearts,
unravelling the bandages of their emotional scars of pain.

Be by their sides in need of therapy.
Communication gives them clarity of past experiences.
holding back, they will want to do so,
sadness that haunts their heartbreak movie stories.

Hear them out and digest their grief.
Hold them close to you to make them know
you here to fix their crushed home.

Slowly, you waited to place them back together again.
Their walls came down with love.

Those blue eyes

Those blue eyes,
I get lost in those light blue eyes.

There's something deeper underneath your eyes,
they tell so many stories,
like the first sight you have seen
or the first memory you cherish so deeply.

Your eyes aren't just beauty;
they are knowledge, honesty, strength and kindness.

I get lost in those ocean eyes.
I'm deeply Drifting through the tides of your eyes;
I only wish I could go deeper.

I can't wipe your image out of my brain.
I don't know who you are.
All I can say is that you intrigue me every day.

They are only my words,
but I can't keep them in a cage.

Deep blue eyes

I get lost in those blue eyes,
those deep blue eyes.

There's so much more beneath,
like the sea.

I get lost, drifting through the tides of those blue eyes;
I only wish I could dive deeper.

Your eyes tell so many stories,
like the first memory you cherish so deeply.

Your eyes aren't just beautiful
but are honest and kind.

They are blue like the ocean and crystal lakes,
blue like the sky, so calm and graceful,
blue like an aquamarine stone, clarity of mind,
blue like a morpho butterfly, hopeful, and transformative.

These are just my words,
but I can't keep them in a cage.

Your eyes are more than beauty;
they are blue with an angelic gaze.

APPRECIATIVE OF OTHERS

Thankful for you

When breathing was tough,
you produced the oxygen
for my lungs to have a second chance
to exert the thoughts about how I felt.

When life came crashing down
over my safe place
you were my support beam
to hold myself upright, to look for guidance.

When I was about to explode in frustration,
you were right there to defuse
my emotional reactions.

Never thought to be so attached
to those people who made an impact,
life course changed without a doubt.

As your existence was all that matters,
I dedicate my years to you:
fellowship, partnership, then pursued,
hand in hand,
we changed the aspect of these derelict lands.

You Showed me

You may be gone, but you left me here on this earth
with the hope I would find who I am—
who I'm supposed to be.

You may be in absence, but you showed me
how fun and sad times can be.
You told me never to give up on who I am.

Furthermore, you told me family was everything
even in your last days.

You may be gone, but you will always live inside of me,
as you are a part of me as I am of you.

I love you for not only showing me how to hold on,
but also, to grow.

You showed me love when I needed it the most.
You showed me kindness when I was at my worst.

I love you; I'll always need you, and I'll always miss you.

You showed me first.

Helpers' voices

Call out to the world,
as good hearts will be nearby
to bring you advice
on how to cope.

Setting your issues aside,
calming your mind,
voices of reasoning will bring
peace to your ears.

Stranger, I bumped into

Market shopping
on Saturday mornings were usual for me.

Cappuccino from my favourite mug,
toast and eggs for breakfast
before I set off to see the ingredients
I'll need for afternoon tea.

Aisle Shopping in the centre of London Town,
with the fresh aroma of bakery goods
was a delight to my senses.

As I walked around and didn't see anyone,
I suddenly bumped into the stranger
who eventually meant everything to me.

I apologised for my impolite behaviour,
so casually the stranger said to me.
"It's okay, you did it accidentally."

From then on,
we introduce ourselves,
hours spent still in that same Aisle
exchanging stories of our
important memories.

A life lesson was learned from,
a stranger who became much more.
I thank myself for serendipitously
bumping into you.

Second chance

Given the opportunity,
for reinvention,

As the malfunctions
occurred,
causing a glitch in our systems,
separating us as working
partnered functions.

You gave me the tools
to fix the problems
caused by
viruses in my programming.

The stories that were written
by me always led to
horrific places at the end of conversations.

You gave me
the typewriter
to rewrite the script
of the unfortunate ending.

Rejoiced I came to be
a second chance place along me,
not taken lightly,
as the road to healing
begins.

Dealing with conflict

Put aside our differences,
we lost countless hours through
our emotional trauma.

An exchange of words was heard
in lover's tongues' outburst—
fights of love were powerful,
it shattered all lines of communication
between both of us.

Times we spend separated
birth the realisation that we need each other.

For you and I complement each other's personalities,
the loneliness we filled together.
Attractive forces keep us magnetised.

Through our discussions, we reconcile
by understanding our points of view,
love grows stronger
to clear out our bruises.

Family and Friends

Much more needed on this earth,
family members and friends
are worth more than the wealthiest of wealthy.

For good fortune they bring,
never trade it for diamonds, emeralds or golds,
nor power. Above all,
those are the things that can corrupt us all.

Seek value and happiness through the joint
chains of thoughts.

My dear friends and family
are the strings attached to my heart's instrument to play
songs of solidarity.

Kiss

My lips on your body,
it was a sign of the unbreakable law.

Love was marked by my kiss
on you.

Protected, I will make you so,
forever kindness displayed
around your existence.

Until my body returns to ashes.

Heart Beats

Drums of importance
plays songs for humankind.

No place for wrong notes,
as we are all synchronised.

If one heartbeat fades,
the semitone will be lowered
to play the minor chord notes.

Thus, sad songs are to be composed.

8.1 billion hearts are needed to survive.
Hearts and trumpets are played
to remember what's the significance of Life.

A young heart grew

Travel, young soul.
on a journey of uncertainty.

I came crashing down on a place
I will soon call home.

Once, a little sprout with chains across his mouth,
a broken heart and a silent voice.

The love they showed
gave me hope.

From hiding in the shadows
Now dancing in the sunlight,

I care for each one of them,
little Folks
and the giant ones that kept me close.

As I soon realised, my empty heart slowly grew.
The smile I once lost came back so naturally.

My young heart grew.
I thank the place I landed on.

Not truly gone

I miss your physical presence and the way you hold me so close with a single touch of your fingers
The laughter from your voice the warmth of your lips when you give me kisses, the look in your eyes when you heard the proud words from the news that I had delivered, I miss you more than you can imagine. The long and painful life journey without you as my companion by my side is hard. You may not be with me physically anymore, but the life lessons and memories we shared for years are embedded in my brain, body and soul Your hands are across my shoulders to guide me through the right path of life; it's never a goodbye, but merely a see you later. You're never, ever truly gone

Animal Therapy

They stay with you
no matter where you go.

The bond ships shared through all
those countless licks and shakes
of fluffy hairs across your clothes.

A Companion of love,
they have chosen to be.

Empathetic body language,
movements caused by
the outcry for support
by you.

My animal friend is
the calming effect
on relieving stress.

Auntie

"Tell me what you want," she told us,
 "So, I will get it by tomorrow."
She never once broke her promises.

Outrageous gifts, unexpected surprises,
she said,
"Pack your bags. We are going on a trip."

Ice skating to bowling,
theme parks to museums,
holidays close by or far away, across the seas.
There was never ever a dull moment with my auntie Cheryl.

Ideas she planned to make us laugh,
her love was so broad and tall like a giraffe.

I miss those days when you used to say,
"My dear nephew, it's going to be okay."
You never really liked hugs, but you
gave me one when I needed it so much.

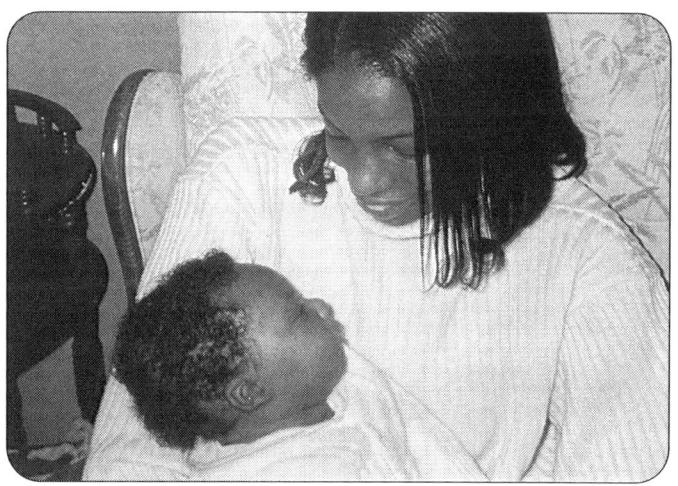

I loved the food you made for us—
spontaneous and delicious meals that we ate and munched.

I choose to remember you before the changes to your life.
I'm saddened that you are no longer here.

Forever loved by the family you left behind,
my auntie's heart grew far and wide.
Here's a poem to let you know,
my dear auntie Cheryl lives on,
even when years pass and go.

Grandma

Portland Francis, people called you that,
however, to me, you were my grandmother.

Rushing home from school again
with the means to kissing you all over again.
Gigantic arms wrapped around you
like you were my teddy bear.

Jokingly annoyed you came to be,
then you utter your favourite phrase "Piss off," to me.
It made me laugh; it made me chuckle,
because we knew you could never be so mean.

Remember the days?
When it was the food, you made?
At that time, I used to hate.
I tried to leave the dinner table to place the food in the bin,
but your eyes stared at my dinner plate.

Until we finished eating the meal,
I begged you for a reasonable deal.
It's gone past 8 o'clock; you're still downstairs,
watching TV through the night, I brought a chair to sit by your side.

You loved to read every time I walked past your room.
I miss your voice,
it's so embedded in my memories.
I'll make you proud,
for eternity, my grandma was everything to me.

REINSURANCE OF SELF-LOVE

Who you are

If you know who you are,
no one can ever hurt you.

As long as you know who you are,
you will always be loved.

The perspective of others should not matter.
If they don't see your true intentions,
you don't need the validation
from anyone else but yourself.

You are so amazing.
The presence of you is a gift in this world,
and I gladly welcome you with open arms.

Who you are should be important to you.
Don't be afraid of yourself, my friend.
Be you.
Stay you.
Love you,
the way, I love myself enormously.

I hope one day you can do the same.
Be proud to be you.

Stay calm

Calm breathes throughout the land,
with one noise of heartbeats standing.

I hear the sweet sounds of the blue whale's charms.
Stay slow and steady; you're going to be fine.

Remember the moments when you chuckled?
The last thing you accomplished—
great applause erupted in the world's ears
when you performed God's wonders.

Enough overthinking,
deep, slow breathing for clearness.
Listening to the calming sounds of silence.

Simply breathe

Deep breaths, no stress.
Remember to breathe.

Please stay alive with me.
Just simply breathe.

I'm good enough

Good enough to breathe,
good enough to live among humankind.

Useless you never were,
a lost person in a field
who finally escaped from pain
that kept their wings grounded for years.
Took flight for the first time.

Your laugh matters more every day
when you let it show,
letting go of all your insecurities.
The way your presence in me
makes me glow with warmth.

I found my value inside myself
and not from others.
The inner seeking of happiness
tells me that I'm good enough
to just accept,
you were born to be unique.

Don't come back

I trusted you with my heart,
my secrets,
only to be hurt by your duplicity.
My heart is empty, with holes filled with tears.

I wonder if anything ever mattered to you—
the poems,
the encouragement,
the gifts or the validation you didn't need.

I put my love on the line for you,
only to be hurt by the disguise of the words you say.

So, love another, but don't come back.
My love is special, and you never deserve the chance you had;
you missed it to know me, so please don't come back to try.

I'm worth more plus the oath I must uphold.
I will continue to love myself,
for this door has permanently closed.

Value you

I see the value in you,

Victorious, you will be.

Appreciated by what you are,

Loved by thousands but also loved by you.

Universe so big but you're all that matters.

Accepted for who you are, nothing less.

Yes, to being you.

Obtain self-happiness.

Unforgettable, you're destined to be.

Mirrors

The reflection of what stands in front of me
is a confusing figure of unusual properties.
Their eyes were watering down
or sometimes lighting up
through their happiness or sorrow.

I got lost through the forever-changing
cycles of my reflections
through the Years of ageing—

A sort of mirrors that is the abstract of
my different personalities,
that is all a part of me,
scattered throughout.

The type of structured mirrors,
rather, a clear picture painting
or a cracked-up painting. For many
types of mirrors I stood in front.

The reflection I want to see
is one of certainty, of hopes of a better future.
My
definite mirror will reflect
the person I will grow
to love and behold.

MY SOUL

Floating in a space
in between my chest,
lays a force so powerful
unseen by the naked eye.

Hand placed over my chest,
going around in circular motion,
three taps along
my sternum—

It awakens a great surge
of purpose,
full of breath,
ignited flames.

Combined with DNA,
here was the resting
place of the beauty
of my humanness.

When I was young

Dear young me, I hope you're still happy.
I hope you enjoy staying with your family,
running home from school for nothing more
than giving your grandma a hug,
excited to see what our auntie had planned next.

I hope you still care about our dreams,
outside rolling through mud, running through rain,
the feeling of the ground when you lay down
to see the clouds and guessing what shapes they make.

I wonder if you still love playing with our brother,
even though we tease each other.
The trips we went on for nothing more
then enjoyment.

Young me, I hope you love every moment
of being a silly little kid with no worries.
I wish to go back to those times.
life has changed, and I hope you don't have to experience it so soon.

My young dear me,
cherish every single moment.

Ghost

Do you know how it feels
to walk among the souls as a ghost,
not to be seen or heard?

I felt this for years.
No one saw me.
No one cared for me.

Do I exist?
Do I breathe?
Or am I just another machine
in people's eyes?

I saw the way they looked at me;
their eyes were like a void,
and I'm just a casket with nothing inside,
only darkness that covers the light.
Is this the reason why I can't be seen by the eye?

Many times, I thought people acknowledged me,
but they just saw straight through me.
I'm a broken statue with no value.
My heart feels like stone.

I'm a human too,
and I'm worth the same value as you,
so don't act like you don't see me too.

Do you know how it feels
to be forgotten about for years?

I had to find a way to change myself
to gain that crown and be that person,
the number one.

So, everyone could see me.
So, everyone could cheer me on.

But I don't change.
I don't fake; I'm going to stay the same.

Forget what you people have to say.
Because I'm not going to be a ghost no more.
I'm going to be heard.
I'm going to be seen.

There's no ghost in me.

HEALING AND HEALING FROM HURT

●

Better days ahead

Every day, there's a sunrise,
of new hopes and possibilities.

Yesterday's pain has been eradicated,
from my brain as I sleep and dream-
the dreams that will become reality
with the greatest goal of mankind:
to surpass the past civilisations of history.

Challenges faced in this era of the present world
will be conquered by the new generations
enlightened by common
knowledge of past failures.

Better days are ahead for you,
my dear ones.

Music of happiness

The sounds of happiness
come in waves of joy.

Like a rollercoaster,
it mirrors your highs and lows.

The simple notes of music are a spectacle.
I love its storytelling through words and imagery,

The yelling and screaming of hurt and empathy,
the shine of vocal cords
dancing through your earlobes.

Songs I relate to are mine and yours.
Music is healing for my mental thoughts,
a medicine for stress,
a medicine for growth.

My music of happiness is an
endless road.

Stories of overcoming struggles

Take sips from a coffee mug,

as we are only on a new chapter.

Past events of life's status
is not one's to fault over.

For you're in the stages of the falling actions,
the part of your story dedicated to solving problems.

Struggles were in the past
due to Resolutions.

A story you're shaped into,
life's great ending.
Began through changes in
journeys' developments.

My quiet place

My place of mellow,

In peace, which follows
the calmness of my heart.

Beats for self-liberation,
vibrations sent through my body
in quiet feels from the universe.

My pleasure is natural beauty,
a quiet sound around me.
Thoughts on living was clarified
to me, though, the ears of quiet.

Simplicity, a place of quiet, is dear to me—
recharged energy was made for me.

Importance

Yesterday will be forgotten in history,
and today will be remembered in the future.

I'm in control

For voices that interrupt
the Great resting peace
in mind, stand clear of
the platform as my
expedition is only one step forward.

In absolute freedom of expression
bad decisions were left at the station.
The station that once controlled me
I left behind full-heartedly with no
regrets when boarding my train
on the way back to positivity.

Promise of tomorrow

Sunrise is eternal,
blue skies relish, birds of paradise
soaring to great heights.
Green life blossoming into earth's colours,
swaying the healing notes of nature's tunes.

Sea waves gently, warmly touch against my skin,
I feel myself on an astral plane.
Lights of blistering gold dust on a journey of life,
waked up reborn, as I am a Phoenix.

Tomorrow is an adventure.
with unexpected events.
I promise today will be better than yesterday.
If promises don't work, I close my eyes.
Time reverts to the moment of sunrise.

Meditation

Forms of Meditation are often
used to improve your mental health,
by taking action to improve yourself.

Yoga mats placed in Great Gardens,
satisfaction acquired through
growing over your inner darkness.

Concentration on hopes of future,
love for the person you will become.
Unhappiness was an afterthought.

Awareness and meaningfulness
came with a stable state of calmness.
I closed my eyes to repeat this,
experience of therapeutic meditation.

The senses of realisation

Awaken the mind of your full potential,
to your soul-born purpose.

Enlightenment has arrived past the horizon of self-doubt.
Calmness has settled through,

The sounds of hummingbird's tweets,
steady steps along the river.

Rehydrate the idea of the place
you intend to go.

Greatest consumed by the
dreamers of tomorrow.

Who Fought Against
voices of demons.

To overcome their fears.
a sense of peace was embedded

in their souls entirely.

Free beings grew into the person
they strived to be.

A new meaning to relish,
influencing your life.

Nothing that made sense to you
became the most powerful thing.

The gift of realisation is yours.

Perfume senses

The smell of scented air
across the necks of those-

Who inspired to create
their own empowerment
within themselves.

Not to be impressed
by others,

nevertheless, they are not afraid
to share their self-esteem

by the changes in their body chemistry
through personalised scent
of boosted self-confidence.

Apply it to the skin
of healing properties,
breathing in the forms
of noble energy.

Shower feelings

Hot water is the product
that cleanses doubt, upon yourself.

Warmth-waters touch then enhances
the belief of Soothing remedies.

Showers above your head
are raindrops' hydration—

The way of functionally
beginning by absorbing
the feelings of relaxation.

Home

This place is one of security,
the coping mechanism for my anxiety.

This is the only sacred place of mine,
my heart is drawn by its aura

of utter peace, empowered by
the cemented walls of rehabilitation

within the mindset that flows
on streams, quiet lake waters.

My home is where
the waterfalls of healing herbs flow

Through the prosperity of life,
which continuously grows.

Fight for

Awake is where I want to be,
breathing is my energy.

Worthy love was
chosen to be consumed,

as death was now in
my rearview mirrors.

Another chance to lay
eyes on what's important,

the things which needed guarding,
memories worth cherishing,
people worth valuing.

By Holding on to the chains
of the very thing that confined you,

and climbing out occurred when
you decided to choose the path of

fighting for the future of your life,

the burden which you
placed across yourself,

in hopes of feeling better.

Change

Beautiful metamorphosis
that happens in all of us

Through times and circumstances,
it was a process of healing.

The changes through the air,
that fondly graces your heart,

are realisation that you are almost there,
a better you are out on the horizon.

Forgetting the reasoning of sadness
in the first place,

The changes of your characteristics
mark the completion of your healing journey.

Keep going

I feel your pain in many ways,
I feel the beat of your broken heart.

I see the light fading from your eyes,
from the sunny skies.

In loss, we smile to hide the pain.
in the days to come, it slowly fades away,
blowing sands of the hourglass.

I know you're going through a lot—
loss of words and emotional thoughts,
mixed feelings and anger at the world
for hurting someone that you love.

I know words aren't enough to change the hurt,
that bleeds deep throughout the cloth.
Unexpected news that ruins one's view.

But don't give up hope, as I will not.
Love is strong, and evil is not.

So please don't give up. Things change and get better,
like when it rains, and the sun comes out to change the weather.

You're there, light. Remember that to get through this difficult time.
It's going to be hard, and you will want to cry,
but you are strong, and you will be revived.

Their memories will give you the power to battle through;
the love they showered is endless time.

Remind yourself of the memories you shared
that no one knows—that smile of yours when they hold you close.

To get through this,
keep going strong. Keep positive thoughts.
Keep the way you love.

From heaven, they look down,
free from pain and sleeping well waiting for birth again.

Proud of what you have done,
for they live in you eternally.

So don't say bye, as it's just a new page
with unwritten stories to be shared again.

When you reunite with your loved one on that special day,
you can't wait to tell them more about the life you lived.

So, keep on going brave.

From Pain to Love | Words of Love

MOTIVATION AND LOOKING FORWARD

Climbing mountains

Life is full of mountains,
which you must conquer.

There will be challenges along the path,
blocking the view from the sunlight's goals.

The tribulations of the past
will give you the power to persevere
and hike through the conditions
of each mountain's trials.

Learning

Learning through every life lesson and every experience,
from seconds to minutes to hours to days to weeks to months to years,
will make you
unbreakable for the rest of your entire life.
Chapter to the end of knowledge's minds,
remember this learning lecture until the moment you die.

Live freely

Celebrations and triumphs
thus, heartbeats grow far
eyes closed in wonder

Trials in grand motion
embraced by our sparks
the adventures of life with
no regrets in our hearts

Lived on experiences
by owning our minds
a lifestyle was chosen
to live independently

from thus on
a dove was then
set free.

Happiest

The pain that I once indulged in
came flushing out of my system.
Happiness was chosen
for the rest of my life.

Sunshine and rainbows
guided me through
the bridges of smiles.

The new joyful memories
lived even longer than
the previous ones.

Changes kept
blossoming
across my heart's veins.
branches grow upwards,
pumping one's energy anew.

A chain reaction then followed,
by travelling through
the yellow brick road.

New year

Year past of this emotional rollercoaster,
fireworks in-light of changes coming,
brightening up the even darker
night skies.

My life will flourish
in this new year of transfiguration.
slates within the past year have been
cleared by the waters of new.

I choose this year to be
my new beginning.

Life goals

Life is about perusing something better.
if you are not happy with what you have today,
only you can take the initiative to change.

Start by going out for a run.
Start by smiling at a joke you thought of in your head.
Start by saying you're okay, by looking through the mirror.

You're my reflection, which I must look after.
I'm a parent on this grand adventure.

Start by greeting those who love you dearly.
Hugs and kisses warm my heart.

Ready to be set free,
my life is right in front of me.

So spread your wings, little butterfly.
Chase your dreams and life goals.
You will score with me.
I promise you will succeed.

Noted lists ticked off by you,
you lived life to the fullest.

Little Birds

Little birds, why do you stay?
Born to fly so take flight.
Discover heights and feel the wind by your side,
blue-sky mornings and starry nights.

Mother has guided you all through your early stage of life.
I think you're worried about
what the world has to offer,
scared by the unknown,
by dangerous beings with blackness within their souls.

Your mother's knowledge is all you know.
Let this be a lesson for growth and development.
Let you find what makes you happy,
catching up with each of the earth's wonders.

I see the change in your little eyes
full with ambition to become much bigger.
so little birds, spread out your wings—
there's so much more than the surface you stand on.

Chase it through the winds.
My little birds are now conquerors of the sky.

Dance

The movements
created by my beloved
body Language Were
indeed, to inspire others.

The dance of a century
released the forgetfulness
about your worries.

As at this moment,
the weight of
expression
meant everything.

Journey of a patient snail

I'm a snail, not here to run.
I'm a snail, not here to cheat.
I'm a snail, not here to beg.
The word rapid is not associated with me.

Unnecessary pressure weight is cut down.
Take your time; it is the only start of your life.

I'm at a steady pace in my development.
My journey will eventually take me to
an even better place.

The word believe is the key
for this integral life race.

Snail was my nickname
across the whole country,
as being patient
was okay
to me.

Decision

Choices made by many,
destinies written or changed.
A risk on a tightrope is walked,
mental notes written down.

I remember when life was easy,
no care for bruises,
enthusiastic flowers dancing down the stream.

Now life's changing, for better or for worse.
Wrong moves made by hurting another
by doing something for yourself.

I hate how decisions can affect your health.
For better or for worse,
I decided on happiness.

My purpose

Born with the burden,
in the later stages of life, I've seen
in helping others to see their true needs.

Careful truths I let release,
my thoughts are woven to clear out negativity,
patching up misguided thoughts through lucidity.

My body shakes in surges of energy from painful
waves of tears and agony,
heard by my ears from distressed
low-spirited souls.

I hope to heal everything,
a love so strong
to bring light
of guarded care.

BRINGS YOU JOY
AND IN LOVE WITH

Midnight Drive

Street lights across the night skies,
the buildings of great art
were visible from the cars,
the cars that journey through the cities.

With no destination in mind,
but the never-ending road is in sight.
The music playlists that were made
with the intentions of those who felt the same energy
as yours.

The free spirits dancing through the night,
singing from the top of their lungs.
The hands reaching out the windows
felt the airwaves through their fingertips.

Nothing else matters but the drive,
the best nights of your lives,
we were driving through the midnight hours.

Rain

Laying on my bed,
taping of my bedroom windows,
gloomy afternoon.

Book reading through the storm,
rain drops hit my therapy tunes.

When rain pours, for some, it's like every sad story,
of crying tears.

I love rain.
It's the sound of meditation.
Clearing the drops of pain from rivers' dulcet gifts,
deep in thoughts of soothing relief
from little clatters along the rooftops.

Rain, more from dark clouds along the sky,
spread sprinkles on the ground in hopes the plants will grow.
Rain more for the earth will go to show
beautiful growth.

Light

Guided by ignited curiosity,
lights of hopefulness
that shines throughout
the world, even in the
smallest areas of darkness.

We look over it to understand it,
thus, its worthiness to captivate us Closer.

The light that burns brightly in all of us
is our morality,
our purity of cosmic energy.

Lights and glowing graces
conquered the darkness
for happiness and prosperity.

Remember, there's light in all of us,
even the smallest sparks of light
are important to be shown.

Faith

Faith is the dove that
flies in the highest skies,
clouds that produce
the purest airwaves of singularity.

I've seen it at the dawn before sunrise,
across the world's phenomena.
Faith tangles within creation
of the spiritual dimension of the
heart, soul and mind.

The tears that are shed don't last forever,
like the loss of a life.
Faith is blowing out of birthday cake candles,
in hopes your wishes come true.

I've heard it through sways of trees,
the acts of kindness
committed by those
who healed those wounds,
from opening by words of truth
through misery.

I see that there is faith calling out
for me to be welcomed in.

Flowers

Flowers are beautiful
for not just the way
they look and by how
they stand.

Air of virtue
they give us,
thus lands
we perch on,
is there in growth.

Joy and pleasure,
It's smell of Love
Is liberated
Through the
Seeds of the flowers,
Producing world's peace.

A flower of acclamation.

Story books

I do long for those books on my shelves,
with many stories written within them.

I get lost through the pages,
travelling to landscapes of imaginative places.

I do wonder where I'll be going next.

Chair

A chair is close to you,
a chair that will listen to you,
for it sees your emotional complexities—
your happiness and sadness.

A chair that keeps your secrets close,
a place where you feel at home,
a chair that holds you tight
when time gets hard for the 100th time.

It's old and brittle, but it holds itself up strong,
because it knows how important it is to you.
The memories shared that you don't even know,
it sees the other side of you
that the world doesn't see.

A chair that stays when you're not at home,
but is there when you're on your own.

This chair is sacred to me alone.
As soon as I was born, I was placed
across your soul,
a thinking place for my mind to be at rest.

A chair that weighs so much more along
my chest.

Dreams of the night

Nights of sleep are
a place of tranquillity,
it's the creative power,
an open source of eternal possibilities.

A canvas so expansive for your creative minds,
dreaming is the gift of escaping
from the reality of pain.

The safety boxes
on the expressive floor.

Beds are the first step towards a
transformative Peace Movement,
the smiles of those who enter
once their eyes have closed.

Imagination is so extraordinary and is the final step into
those dreamy nights.
Happiness shines through
the window glass on the other sides of nightmare's crimes.

My nights are spent in
the dream world of
enjoyment.

Travel Bugs

I travel time to time
for new discoveries,
to see the world not through a telescope
but up closer, you can see the fine detail prints unfold.

Countries of different cultures
and diverse environments,
I get lost staring out my plane view window.
Noting in my mind
how these lands came to be.

I thank this expansive world
to be able to gain knowledge
from over the seas.

I love the excitement of where
I might be heading next.

There's so much more to explore.
I'm just a little bug on this gigantic adventure.

Rome

The sights of the wonders of Italy's streets,
the open stores are filled with the aroma of coffee beans
and fresh breakfast cuisine.

Firefly lights are lit up on the streets at night.
Looking through all the restaurants,
pasta and pizza with red wine were the best choices for all.

Walking around in this city of art,
with the kindness of people not so far behind,
there were adequate buildings from centuries ago,
brilliantly chiselled by umarell workers.

The structures were miraculous,
from piazza Venezia to piazza di Spagna
from Saint Peter's Basilica
to the Vatican museums,

Football stadiums but most Importantly, the Rome Colosseum.

Time well spent there gathering knowledge,
to Rome, my heart belongs.

My favourite summer

My favourite summer of 2013,
I wish most days I could go back to.

The summery breeze,
Staying up all night,
Table tennis and bike relay races
With the neighbourhoods' favourite kids.

Summer is the exchange of partial
Tears of reflection on our
Saddest days, then looking forward to
The happiest of the brightest moments of our pointed gaze.

Astonishment through our eye lenses,
For the moment, the earth opened its arms to show
The summer displays.

I remember what summer meant to me.
When it comes around to say hi again.

Autumn

My favourite time of year is
when the orange and brown colours appear.

The leaves that once were green are now yellow, orange and red.
The leaves that fall off the trees to grace the winds of autumn presence
the conkers that have been made for collection,
to please the squirrel's hungry stomachs.

I love the continuous pour of rain.
When I'm walking with my umbrella
through the park of autumn days,
the stop on a park bench
to read through my books is
gently relaxing, filled of pleasure,
with the lake in front of me.

A warm furnace back home,
with Starbucks tea to keep me company.
As I gaze on my autumn
list of movies and tv shows
to get me through these autumn nights.

I love to decorate my house with
Halloween decorations
to get ready for Octobers arrival.
Candles lit around my apartment,
the true beauty of autumn is finally here.

Walking through the park

Green life lives in these landscapes,
countless colours of cherished trees and plants,
which was enlightening to me.

The buzzing noise from down below
were the grasshoppers of the world's
small creatures.

Walking through my calming place
by riverside,
I glanced across the horizon of the lake.
Swimming fishes gently glide past the water waves.

Thoughtful thoughts
come into fruition with being
one with nature.

Dogs and their owners
playing games with tennis balls.
While young children running around the park
with nothing to be worried about at all.

I love walking through my park, as you will
never know what you might find
when you arrive for another visit
in the next period of time.

I miss you, early 2000s

2000s, I do miss you dearly,
I remember you fondly from the memories
placed inside my time capsule.

The clothes that we used to wear—
denim pants, coloured shirts, and those baseball caps.
Shoes of early brands' life cycles.

I remember those giant, big phones with the aerials,
the ones that flip open,
the indestructible brick phones.

Disposable cameras and handheld camcorders,
which were used to capture images and videos of our youth.

I miss those early 2000s movies that were iconic for so many,
the teen best dramas of popularity,
the twins who were high within this industry.
I remember a certain redhead girl
who was in all your favourite movies.

I love the soundtracks to all those stories,
playlist made by me in thoughts of those.

I miss the early 2000s for all those classic
cartoon shows that I grew up on.

My heart belongs to the 2000s.

My love for the movies

Join the escape of reality,
as you leave your worries behind in the other world,
the world of so much pain.
Join me in this new chapter, the big story
that lies across the cinema screen.

The thoughts of wonders that bleed through my eyes of imagination
as I see it evolve into a masterpiece.
I love the impactful scenes of characters talking to one another with tension in the air,
the audience holding tightly to their chairs
and inching slightly closer with each word exchanged between characters.

The actions scenes that have my full attention,
and the moments that are stained within my brain.
I love the background music, which is the thread
and the needle that stitches a scene together to give it more depth.

But most importantly,
I love how movies are never the same; they can be hopes and dreams,
but they can also show the reality of the world around us.
Movies are important to be seen.

Dis/Ability

Got nothing more than an ability, don't look at them differently.
Getting by from dawn to dusk is a normality for us.
A constant request for help, it was outrageous to discuss,
for you and I are the same no matter what had hindered us,
because we both share a connected humanity and equality.

So please don't look at them differently.
We all have our own disabilities,
we can proudly show
when it's time for the world to finally grow out.

Thoughts of division in hopes of a true vision,
my dis/ability was a gift, a courtesy,
a blessing which was trusted by the perspective of your gated keys,
to outgrow your inner insecurities.

Enjoy what you choose to keep.
My dis/abilities don't define me.

Skin colours

Shades were made but not to discriminate.
I love different types of shades as we make up
our universal umbrella of our different
cultural races and ethnicities.

Different ways of living mean many more ways of learning.
Prejudice and stereotypes were left at the door;
racial slurs and racial malice were unacceptable actions to do at all.

Don't just look at people for their colour,
as I choose to see them as a whole.
I know there's pain within your skin from all those years ago;
however, you must change the narrative for all,
skin colours are beautiful,
which includes mine and yours.

Skin colour is more than the barricade,
as underneath is
where the real human being lays.

Late night conversations

Long conversations were like a
continuous spiral of possibilities,
from one topic to the next,
our task was to stay up late.

Taking a hiatus from sleeping,
effortlessly it came to be,
resonating through conversation,
understanding how time was a
concept we attended to escape from.

For clock watching never crossed our minds.
From the darkest hours to the dawn of light,
I related with someone on a level unfathomable
to explain.

Your eyes

Your eyes are different to mine.
not just the colour of our eyes,
our eyes are left for interpretation.

We see things differently.

There are old eyes, new eyes upon the Earth,
eyes that have seen everything,
and
eyes yet to gaze upon the Earth.

We see things differently because
we need to, we have to.
As our eyes hold up the alluring
truth of our earth's captivating stories.

Everlasting time

Time is not just the past, present, or future.
Time is unique.

Time is moments;
time is a capsule of emotional beginnings and ends;
it is light and darkness;
it is ups and downs.

Time is where memories are created and forgotten in history.
Time is where life is born and where life is ended.

With time, there is growth in one as a person.
With time, there is understanding in others,
to know not only their pain and suffering,
but also, their hopes and dreams.

Time allows us to create a real entwined chemistry between one another,
to push forward and become a better version of ourselves.

Everlasting time is the love language of generations.

Realisation you have love and happiness Afterall

In order to find love and happiness,
you must take a second,
a deep breath and widen

your vision binoculars,
your mind capacity and heartbeat drums.

To find that those very feelings of
love and affections of happiness
are all around—

Even by appreciating
the smallest ones and realising it's
always been with you,

you will have
absolute proclivity into finding more.

Signs of art love

If art love is a story in a picture, I haven't finished yet.

Small detailed strokes across my empty canvas
with hopes of showing art love in different forms.

The buildings of old that lasted centuries
were windows in time for the world's history.

The famous monuments across countries
that hold some special significance and moments of beauty.

Great museums of wisdom's gifts
are the knowledge of kingdoms from beginning to end,
and citizens of all ages who chose to change their ways
for a better way of living.

The bookstores of endless stories along old walls
holding the residences of authors devoted storytelling,
allow you to be transported into worlds of your imagination
to get lost in without the stresses that you face.

The special moments of life, from birth to adulthood,
from your first words to the smallest moments of happiness,
the couples that have lasted years together
with their love growing every single day.

I see art in all things.
Emotional, physical,
objects, and subjects too big for one picture.

Art love is all around us.
it just depends on how you see it and feel it.

For my lost bright stars that need help

If you have been truly affected or been resonated with a poem and are looking for help but find it difficult to turn to anyone, I deeply encourage you to get out of feeling your alone which I personally felt for years after the loss of both my grandmother and aunt. I hid away how I was feeling and carried on with my goal of helping others without ever thinking of putting myself first which I finally realise and understand It's completely okay to do and seek support while still continue to help others later on. You matter, and so does your voices. It can be hard to express how you feel, when especially you feel or seem like no one would truly understand, or when you're unsure of your own emotions. But please believe me, my bright stars, there are people who can help bring out your voice, your heart, and your light. They're here to guide you towards healing and happiness. If you feel like the light inside of you is dimmed and you need the correct support, don't ever once hesitate to reach out. Pursue the best version of yourself, because you are honestly amazing even if you don't see it yet, and if your star still shines brightly and want to help others, here's a list of numbers you can call. For my dimmed stars, if you need someone to listen when your family and friends may not be enough to dealing with the things you are going through. I whole heartly and hope this encourages you to take that first step toward healing and rediscovery of the love for yourself and the things that makes you happy.

UK numbers

Drug addiction: 0300 123 6600
Porn addiction: 0207 935 5333
Alcohol addiction: 0300 123 1110
Gambling addiction: 0808 8020 133
Mental Health: 0800 58585858
Self-harm: 116 123 or 0800 068 4141
Cancer support: 0808 808 00 00
Human trafficking: 08000 121 700
Domestic Abuse: 0808 2000 247
Discrimination: 0808 800 0082
Homeless shelter: 0808 800 4444
Knife crime: 0808 800 5000 or 0800555111

(If you are out of the Uk, please find the correct numbers that are correlated to the country you are living in)

Dear Readers

Dear readers, thank you from the bottom of my heart for reading my poetry collection. It means the world to me to share this with,

you and I hope you resonated with the powerful messages and meanings behind my poems which tried to convey.

Whether you find yourself on any side of the spectrum of pain or love, my hope is that my words helped your voices to be heard

every single person on this planet is important, and we are all equal, and should be treated them same, no matter

how different we may seem. My name is Ricco Francis, and I love poetry because it allows for raw expression without being confined by the boundaries of Imagination which is limitless. I began writing poetry as a way to cope with the loss of my grandmother and aunt, but soon realised that many others also experience their own versions of pain and suffering, which I wanted to bring to light in this collection. On the other hand, I have always been an emotionally expressive, loving and happy person, eager to help as many people as I can. This led me to also write poems about love for my collection in addition to pain because, while pain may be overwhelming at times, love is stronger, and I believe that everyone eventually returns to the spectrum of love. Finally, I want to remind every soul reading this, that in this world, a star was born to shine just like the rest. Keep shining by doing things that make you happy and brings you joy. And if you are already shining brightly, look for those whose lights may be dimming, and reach out to share your light with them. Everyone deserves the bright light of happiness in life.

With heartfelt gratitude,
Ricco Francis

Acknowledgements

I would just like a second to pay my respects and thanks to the people who had a role, big or small, in pursuing my dream of writing this poetry collection that has meant everything to me throughout the two and a half years of writing it. This journey has been very hard and difficult, but also very rewarding and inspirational, and I wouldn't change a single thing about it, as it has also influenced some of my poetry along the way. First of all, I want to thank my auntie Cheryl and my grandmother Portland for being the two people a grandson and nephew could ask for. You had, and still have, avital and pivotal role in shaping the person I am becoming, and I hope I've made you proud. I Thank you for everything, your love, your care, your hearts, and your beautiful way of showing me different loving gestures. I also want to thank the rest of my family, who have always supported me from the moment of my birth and until now, even as we have all gone through difficult times and circumstances together. We are still always there for one another without question. To my friends, it's hard nowadays to find people who completely understand you as a whole person, and to be able to relate with someone else on a deeper level, but luckily for me, I found a great group of wonderful friends who I also consider my second family. Thank you for accepting me the way I am, and thank you for all those deep, great late-night conversations. You have also had an influence on my poetry. Lastly, I want to thank my second home, Sheen Mount. I would like to thank everyone, past and present, at Sheen Mount for welcoming me in with open arms. At a time when I felt lost and hopeless, I found myself again, along with my purpose on this earth, which is to help and inspire others as much as I can. I am thankful and full of gratitude for every single person I met there, for teaching me amazing life lessons and creating wonderful moments that ultimately led me down the path of rediscovery.

I am truly thankful, I have made lifetime bonds with everyone at Sheen Mount, no matter where life takes me. Overall, I would like to thank every kind soul on this earth for continuously inspiring me to become better and help others where I can.

Many thanks,
Ricco Francis.

Printed in Great Britain
by Amazon

4c505219-53b3-4f3b-9e5d-53b5f6eb877cR01